learn to SPEAK FILM

a guide to CREATING, PROMOTING & SCREENING *YOUR MOVIES*

WRITTEN BY MICHAEL GLASSBOURG

DESIGN & ILLUSTRATIONS BY JEFF KULAK

Owlkids Books acknowledges the financial support of the Canada Council for the Arts, the Ontario Arts Council, the Government of Canada through the Canada Book Fund (CBF) and the Government of Ontario through the Ontario Media Development Corporation's Book Initiative for our publishing activities.

Published in Canada by
Owlkids Books Inc.
10 Lower Spadina Avenue
Toronto, ON M5V 2Z2

Published in the United States by
Owlkids Books Inc.
1700 Fourth Street
Berkeley, CA 94710

Library and Archives Canada Cataloguing in Publication

Glassbourg, Michael
    Learn to speak film : a guide to creating, promoting & screening your movies / written by Michael Glassbourg ; illustrated by Jeff Kulak.

Includes index.
ISBN 978-1-926973-84-5 (bound).--ISBN 978-1-926973-85-2 (pbk.)

    1. Motion pictures--Production and direction--Juvenile literature.
2. Motion pictures--Vocational guidance--Juvenile literature. I. Kulak, Jeff, 1983- II. Title.

PN1995.9.P7G545 2013   j791.43   C2012-907641-4

Library of Congress Control Number: 2012954724

Design: Jeff Kulak

Manufactured in Shenzhen, Guangdong, China, in February 2013, by WKT Co. Ltd.
Job #12CB2749

A   B   C   D   E   F

Publisher of Chirp, chickaDEE and OWL
www.owlkidsbooks.com

LEARN TO SPEAK FILM

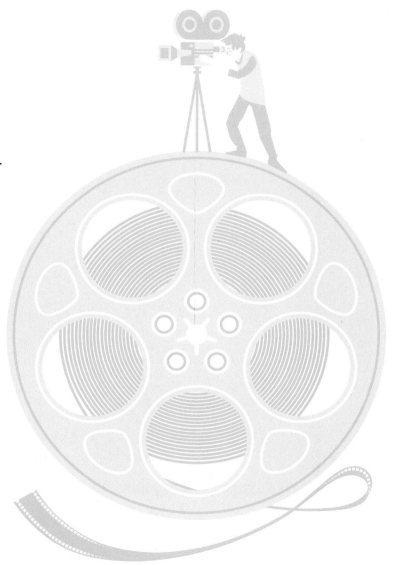

TELLING STORIES WITH PICTURES

Seen any good movies lately? It's a question as common as "What's the weather like?" So what's with this fascination we all have with movies?

Well, for one thing, we love going to the movies! It's a ritual that's been going on for years and years, and we still feel the same excitement today that people felt in the late 1800s, when film began.

The more you learn about film, the more exciting it becomes. In some ways, making films seems like a mysterious process. It's true that a lot goes into making a film, but there is nothing so

complicated that you can't understand it. And we are going to explore everything that goes into making a film.

What fascinates you about film? The actors? The director? The costumes? The music? Where the ideas come from? Everything? Hey, the whole process is exciting.

A big part of this book is exploring what film really is and what people who work in film do. Another big part is showing you how you can make a film yourself, either on your own or with a few friends. Making movies is challenging and sometimes exhausting. But films are a great way to express who you are and what is important to you. And they can be a lot of fun.

A Few Things about Myself

I love to watch movies and I love to make movies. Making movies is like sharing stories with family, friends, and the public. So I've written, directed, and acted in films, stage plays, and radio documentaries. I've worked with a lot of wonderful people: producers, directors, writers, cinematographers, editors, and actors. I've worked from coast to coast, and many places in between. I've also done a lot of teaching. For the past twenty years, I've been teaching film and television production at Humber College in Toronto. Nothing makes me happier than sharing my knowledge and exploring the world of film with my students. There is always something new to learn. I've learned a lot simply writing this book. So let's grab our popcorn, turn the lights down low, and let the magic begin.

CHAPTER 1

Life Is Like a Film

Have you ever had something happen to you, then you told a friend about it, and you both realized that the story would make an amazing film?

Have you also thought, "Well, it would, but that's not going to happen because it's too complicated and confusing." Guess what? It can happen. You can take that story, play around with it, work at it, and make it into a film. It's not impossible. That's how films get made. You just need a little know-how and some basic equipment—not much more than a camera.

You never know when you'll experience something that makes

you say, "That's a film!" or "That's a scene from a film!" Maybe it's just a snippet of conversation you hear while walking down the street. Or perhaps you see something that you know would make a great story and you realize you'd like to share that experience. That's exactly how filmmakers feel.

If you love films, you already know what an engaging scene is. Or how a line of sizzling dialogue sounds. Or what an emotional soundtrack is.

Or what a good story is. All these things are important elements of film. What you might not know is that you can make dialogue, a soundtrack, and a good scene. You have it in you to create something. Actually, you are ready to learn to make your own films right now. All you need is inspiration and guidance. And that's what this book will give you.

Action!

A painting is made by applying various colors of pigment to a surface, like canvas, usually with a frame around it. A sculpture is a freestanding object made out of materials like clay or stone or wood. But what is a film?

Here is the equation:

IMAGES

An image is a visual moment in time. A powerful image causes a reaction in the viewer. One image may mesmerize us with its beauty, while another repulses us. And still another image can have us laughing. The potential reactions are infinite.

Motion can mean different things. It can refer to how things move physically, like people walking, clouds rolling by in the sky, or cars speeding down the highway. It can also refer to how a person's life unfolds. Our lives aren't stagnant, as there are always things happening. If we look at how one event connects to another, and then another, we see that there is motion in everyday events.

Whether a film is comedy, horror, science fiction, suspense, or drama, and whether it is a big or small production, it has the same basic elements in common with most other films: images and motion.

What's So Special?

Years and years ago, when humans were mostly hunters and gatherers, people would sit around a campfire after a long day. When everyone was seated and hushed, someone would tell a story.

An elder might tell a fable about the beginning of the universe or a tale to frighten and amuse the children. While the stories were told, no one would move or make a sound. The audience was entranced because people have always loved to be entertained.

TODAY'S CAMPFIRE

What event today can have five hundred people assembled in a dark room with their cell phones turned off, not talking or moving for two hours or more except to spontaneously laugh, cry, scream, or mumble "Wow"? A film, of course.

The POWER of FILM

A film can hook us in many ways:

WITH IMAGES AS BIG AS EVEREST

If we are in a movie theater, the images and the people are huge. A face in close-up is gigantic, and we see every bit of it. Every emotion is amplified.

BY SURROUNDING US WITH SOUND

Think of one of your favorite films. Close your eyes. Can you see some images from it? And can you hear what it sounds like? Sometimes the music stays with us as long as the images do. Or the combination of sound and image can be particularly memorable. And when we are surrounded by that music or that sound, it can instantly transport us from where we are to the setting or time period of the film.

BY ENGAGING US EMOTIONALLY WITH FASCINATING CHARACTERS

We so often remember the characters in a film. A fictional character can be as memorable as someone we meet in person.

WITH UNFORGETTABLE STORIES

After we see a movie we love, we rarely forget the story. It stays with us for a very long time.

ON TVS, LAPTOPS, AND CELL PHONES

The film experience varies depending on where you watch. In a theater, everything is big. At home, you can see a film on a smaller screen in a room with the lights on and a few other people, but the magic still works. In fact, it can be fun to enjoy a favorite film in new ways. It's different seeing a horror film alone than with friends. And what's more fun than watching a comedy in a group and laughing together?

IT'S MAGIC

Film brings a world that does not exist to life. Sometimes, it's hard to remember that it's not real. Even though we are clearly in a theater, we suspend our disbelief. If we sit back and examine it, we know that many of the elements we're seeing are fabricated. But our emotions remain thoroughly entrenched in the realities of the film we're watching.

A Cousin to Other Arts

People need to express themselves. We have a need to create and to share. Over the years, we have painted, danced, acted out plays, made music, and written stories. Like these other arts, film meets our need to create and to share.

IT CAN DO ALMOST ANYTHING

There are many art forms. Each has a key element or two that can make it breathtaking for the audience. The dynamics and sheer physical exuberance of dance combine in a thrilling mixture of motion and emotion. With a stirring melody or a rousing rhythm, music can truly touch the soul. A painting can create a striking image that sends shivers down your spine. A photograph can do the same with an image of reality. Literature can grab us and make us deeply involved with the characters.

Film has motion, images, and encourages emotional engagement. The youngest of these art forms, film has evolved quickly—both technically and artistically.

THE ROAD TO FILM

Let's say you decide to take a trip to Rome. You could keep in touch with friends and family by email or text or phone. But 200 years ago, none of these technologies existed. So what would you have done?

You could have made some drawings to share what you saw in your travels. Or written about the experiences. Or waited to see your family and friends and told them about it firsthand. But they could not have seen Rome unless they went there themselves.

PHOTOGRAPHY CAME AND CHANGED EVERYTHING!

With the invention of photography in the early 1800s, people were able to actually show their friends the things they'd seen.

THE FIRST REAL FILMS

The first films were very simple and short—only ten to twenty seconds long. *The Strong Man* (1894) showed a "muscleman" standing in front of a camera flexing his muscles. *The Sneeze* (1896) showed someone sneezing.

THE LUMIÈRE BROTHERS

In France, two brothers, Auguste and Louis Lumière, invented the Cinématographe, a motion-picture camera. That's where the word "cinematography" comes from. The Lumière brothers' first film was *Workers Leaving the Factory* (1895). They simply told the 200 people who worked in their lightbulb factory to walk out the front gates. A few days later, they rented a storefront and projected the film onto a wall. Voilà—the first film in the first cinema.

Film Fest

LET'S GO WAY BACK

The following three films give a sense of what the early film world was like and how the medium has evolved. The first two were made well over a hundred years ago; the third is a modern-day film.

AUGUSTE & LOUIS LUMIÈRE
ARRIVAL OF A TRAIN AT LA CIOTAT

This film is often called the first horror film because viewers sometimes ran out of the theater screaming—they thought the train was actually coming straight for them. It sounds strange, but remember, few people had seen a film before!

GEORGES MÉLIÈS
A TRIP TO THE MOON

This pioneer filmmaker is described as a magician. *A Trip to the Moon* was made seventy years before astronauts landed on the moon.

MICHEL HAZANAVICIUS
THE ARTIST

This is a recent film about the era in movie history when silent films became the talkies. It shows the profound effect that sound and dialogue had on actors and audiences.

INSPIRATION IS EVERYWHERE

Inspiration comes when a person sees something or thinks of something that motivates him or her to begin creating.

An inspired person might barely be able to sit still. That person wants to get to work creating whatever it is that he or she is being compelled to do. For filmmakers, inspiration motivates them to make films.

"WHAT ABOUT ME?"

If you want to learn about film, you need to watch movies. That doesn't sound very difficult. However, watching films to learn from them is a different kind of watching than just sitting back and being entertained. You need to focus and pay attention and be aware of what you are seeing and how you feel about it.

HOW THE PROS FIND INSPIRATION

Professionals need inspiration too. They are constantly watching films. And not just the obvious ones—the blockbusters—but all kinds of films from all over the world. They always search for new visual ideas and new ways of telling stories. When you are looking for inspiration, you are open to everything. Filmmakers don't just watch films. They go to art galleries, attend plays, and do loads of people-watching, which is a great way to do research.

DISCOVERY

You can never know in advance what will inspire you. Go to places you haven't been before: art galleries, plays, concerts. Figure out what you like and what you don't like. More important, articulate why you like something. Why does a story appeal to you? (Perhaps because you learn about yourself and other people.) How is the music you enjoy so much affecting people? (Perhaps because it puts a smile on the face of the entire audience.) What makes visuals appealing to you? (Perhaps you find you especially like the colors of nature.) Go to films you think you'll probably enjoy and even to some you're not sure about. Be fearless—that's what discovery is all about.

EVERYONE HAS A STORY TO TELL

Sometimes you need to look inward for inspiration. You might think your life is boring, but I'll guarantee there is a story there, whether it is real or made-up. Perhaps you already know of a story that could be changed a bit so it makes a good film. Or you might just have heard of an aunt's experience in the armed forces or an ancestor's journey to America. Almost anything can be the basis for a great story—it's all in how you tell it. When you begin to think this way, you are beginning to become a filmmaker.

REMEMBER

Inspiration can come when you least expect it, from anywhere at any time of day: while you are reading the news, watching TV, swimming laps, riffing with a friend, or waking up from a dream. If you are open to inspiration, you will be motivated to create.

Finding Inspiration

Filmmakers often get inspiration from other filmmakers. And sometimes inspiration finds you at the unlikeliest time and lasts forever.

66 For me, watching other filmmakers work is imperative. If it is good, it inspires me creatively and fuels me emotionally. That's the combination that makes me want to create better work. 99

—Don McCutcheon
FORMER PRESIDENT OF THE DIRECTORS GUILD OF CANADA

CHAPTER 2

Through a Lens

You are at a birthday party. The cake arrives. While you reach for your camera, lots of other people also try to capture the moment.

As the candles are being blown out, a flurry of flashes go off as shutter buttons are squeezed. You take a few pictures and turn to enjoy a piece of chocolate cake. Later, when you arrive home, you take a look at the pictures, and they aren't quite what you thought they would be. What you really wanted was to capture the feeling of the party, and specifically that moment with your friends gathered around the cake, all in one frame. But none of your pictures quite do that. You wish you had taken a better picture.

When we take a photograph, it's because we see something that touches us, moves us, excites us: a person, a situation, something. Of course, we want our picture to have the same effect on other people. That is exciting but difficult. Pictures are about emotions—our own and everyone else's.

Photography is a way to express who you are, what you think, and how you see the world. But you need to work at it. You need to figure out how to make the pictures look the way you want them to look. Great photographs come from experimenting, from

making mistakes and learning from them. It is a process that takes time, but you can have a lot of fun along the way. So be patient with yourself. Get used to always having your camera ready. Your camera should become an extension of you; like an arm or a leg, it should always be there. It is your most important tool, so try to learn everything you can about it.

Still photographs are a way to learn about composition, lighting, and most important, what you want to see in your pictures and share with the world.

THE CAMERA AND THE THE EYE

We see things differently than still cameras do. A still camera sees each moment in isolation. But we see things as continuous, connected moments—nothing is frozen alone in time. And unlike a camera, we can look anywhere—not just inside a frame.

FRAMING

The boundary of a photograph is called the frame (like the edges of a painting). The way you place the subject of your photograph within these boundaries is crucial. The framing of your photo can be the difference between one that is OK and one that sings. (A picture that "sings" is really powerful.)

Sometimes you want to frame your subject so that it feels as if the entire universe is in that frame. Usually that means having your subject fill the entire picture so you really don't get a sense of anything else. Sometimes you want to frame your subject so that it feels as if the world goes on and on outside the photograph. Usually that means seeing the subject of your photograph and a lot of other things all at the same time.

ANTICIPATE

Great tennis players seem to know where their opponent is going to hit the ball even before it's off the racket. They are able to anticipate what's going to happen next. Great photographers seem to have a similar instinct for finding exactly the right moment to capture. That's because they too anticipate what is going to happen next. When you are taking photographs, don't just wait for the perfect moment to happen—if you do, you'll have already missed it. The key is to anticipate that moment before it happens.

EXPERIMENT WITH COMPOSITION

Composition is how you arrange the elements in your photograph. It's best not just to point the camera and shoot. Put some thought into how you think things should look. Take the time to find what looks best in the frame. Move the frame to the right, to the left. Experiment. Take the picture from a few different angles.

Perhaps you might cut off your subject or not let your audience see everything. Let people use their imaginations. Other times you may want to get as much in the frame as you can to make people really search for your subject.

HOLD THAT CAMERA STEADY!

This is one of those simple things that's easy to forget. We get excited about an image, so we whip out the camera and shoot. But even if you have an image stabilizer (a device that helps steady the camera), make sure you are standing solidly and motionlessly. Holding your breath when you are about to click the shutter is an old trick that photographers still use.

Try This: Pick up your camera. Go outside. Walk around. Take an entire day and find subjects that attract you. Take pictures of people, landscapes, situations— anything. Enjoy it. At the same time, be aware of how you are framing every shot. Then go home, look at all the pictures you've just taken, and choose three you like. Go back to the spots where you took those pictures and take them again. This time, make them even better in every way you can: control the framing and the composition, and don't forget to anticipate the perfect moment.

Learning from Stills

There is a big relationship between photography and cinematography (page 24). Devon Burns loves doing both.

 You can learn so much about cinematography from taking photos. Taking photos not only helps you understand light, framing, and composing images, but it also helps you become a better storyteller. And that's what cinematographers do: we tell visual stories through composition, framing, and lighting.**99**

—Devon Burns
PHOTOGRAPHER, CINEMATOGRAPHER

Be an Explorer

Being a photographer is like being an explorer. You are discovering what is important to you—that's what you want to photograph. You're also discovering images that are new to you, that are fresh and exciting, and that you may not have considered before.

PICTURE POWER

Get your camera ready, because that's the first step in knowing what kind of images you want to show the world. Now, I don't mean you should take 200 stills of your friends goofing around and then upload them online. That's OK, but you're looking for images that replicate what professional photographers do. You want people to react. You want them to laugh, cry, or be afraid.

The Many Responses to a Photograph

LAUGHTER	COMPASSION	JOY	REPULSION
FEAR	TEARS	ATTRACTION	CONFUSION

WHAT SHOULD I BE LOOKING FOR?

You are looking for what interests you—that's content. You are looking for what looks good—we call that aesthetics.

How do you find these things? Most of the time, you simply walk around with your camera, keep your eyes wide open, and take pictures. Doing this, it's easy to stumble upon something important. A lot of famous and celebrated photographs happened by chance—they could not have been planned. There is a famous photograph of two strangers kissing on the day World War II ended. It only exists because the photographer was in the right place at the right time.

THE UNEXPECTED

In photography, the unexpected can make for a striking photograph. Sometimes you can surprise the viewer by juxtaposing the elements in an image. Like showing a truck filled with chickens passing by a restaurant.

Try This: Now that you have your camera, you need to exercise your shooting eye (we call taking both stills and moving pictures "shooting"). Try to find a subject that would be a juxtaposition of images. In other words, instead of taking a picture of a lovely green valley with rolling hills in the background or an industrial smokestack spewing pollutants into the air, try to take one that has *both* the beautiful pastoral scene and the polluting smokestack. That's an even stronger photograph because of the unexpected pairing of opposite images. Get the idea?

A PHOTOGRAPH TELLS A STORY

These three photographers below are very different, but what they have in common is that their photographs tell stories about their subjects or reveal something unexpected.

GORDON PARKS

Parks documented African-American life in the twentieth century. His body of work also includes fashion photography and photojournalistic exposés.

HENRI CARTIER-BRESSON

Cartier-Bresson was a master of candid photography; he wanted to show life as it is. That means his subjects were never aware that their pictures were being taken.

ANNIE LEIBOVITZ

Leibovitz often takes portraits of celebrities that show them in ways the public has not seen before. You have probably seen many of her photographs in magazines.

Painting with Light

Photographers and filmmakers work hard to get the lighting right for every shot. It's an art. In films, it's called cinematography, which means "painting with light."

WHY NOT JUST SET IT ON AUTOMATIC?

Cameras are smart—they can do almost anything automatically. So they know how much light there is, and they know how to compensate for too much or too little, giving you a similarly lit picture each and every time. But when you light for a specific picture, you can control how it looks. As a photographer, you can control whether a picture looks bright and cheery or dark and threatening.

Aside from mood and atmosphere, lighting can give character to people, and it gives you control over how your subjects look on film.

John Marsonet's Guide to Easy & Effective Lighting

John Marsonet is a cinematographer who believes you can light almost any subject simply and effectively. So here are some simple tips from a pro.

NATURAL LIGHTING: WORKING WITH SUNLIGHT

The sun has all the elements you need for creative lighting. You just have to place both the subject and the camera correctly.

In the Shade

- Compose a shot by placing your subject in the shadow of the sun.

- Now find the setting on the camera that allows you to see the subject clearly—not too dark or too bright. It should look natural to the eye.

On a Sunny Day

- Place your subject facing the camera with his or her back to the sun. Now use a white card to bounce the sun's light onto the subject. (A white card is a large white board—you could use bristol board to start with.)

ARTIFICIAL LIGHTING: WORKING WITH LIGHTS

When we don't use the sun, we need to use lights, but we still want the lighting to look natural. We don't want people to be aware of the lights. The simplest way to get things to look natural is with three-point lighting.

Key Light

This is your main, or "key," light. Try not to place the light directly in front of the subject. This will create "flat" or poor lighting. Instead, light the subject on one side.

Fill Light

This light fills the opposite side, or shadow side, of your subject.

Back Light

This lights the back of the subject. It separates the subject from the background, creating the illusion of depth in your shot.

Tip: Instead of using a direct light on the fill side of the subject, bounce a light onto a white card to fill in the shadows. This will look very natural, like lighting with the sun.

THE IMPORTANCE OF LIGHTING

If a person on camera isn't lit properly, it can look like there were either too many lights or no lights at all.

This is what someone looks like when underlit:

Here's the same person overlit:

And here is that person properly lit:

Film Fest

NOT JUST ILLUMINATION

You might not realize it, but the power of these films comes from the cinematography, or the way they're lit and filmed.

VARIOUS DIRECTORS
HARRY POTTER (ALL OF THEM)

These films use lighting to create mood and atmosphere. We often know the direction a scene will take just from the lighting. Dark and shadowy = danger.

GARY TROUSDALE & KIRK WISE
BEAUTY AND THE BEAST (DISNEY ANIMATED VERSION)

This animated film uses lighting as though it were a live-action film. The characters are lit to look three-dimensional rather than flat, as many animations tend to look.

VICTOR FLEMING
THE WIZARD OF OZ

This is an example of two different lighting techniques together in one film because it shows lighting for black-and-white as well as color.

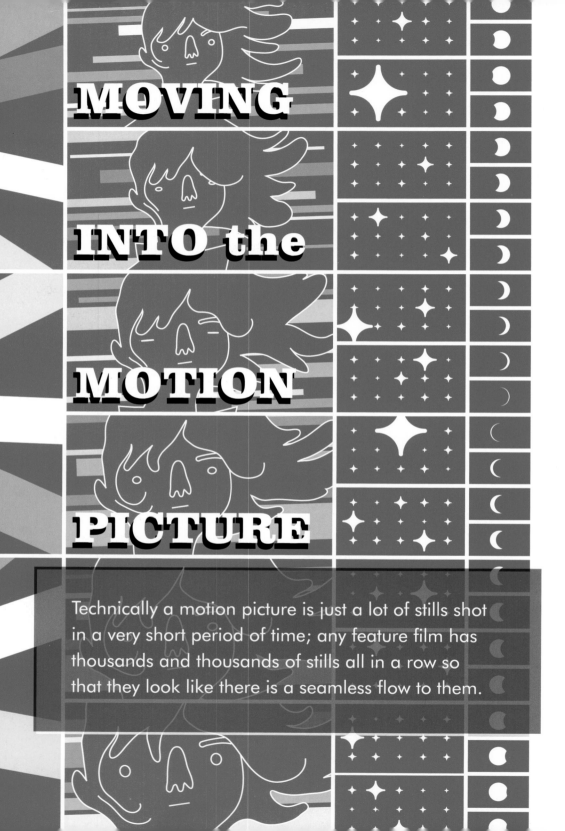

MOVING INTO the MOTION PICTURE

Technically a motion picture is just a lot of stills shot in a very short period of time; any feature film has thousands and thousands of stills all in a row so that they look like there is a seamless flow to them.

TWO KINDS OF MOTION

There is a good reason why regular cameras are called still cameras. While you are taking the picture, the camera must be still, and once you've taken the picture, the frame is still.

With a motion-picture camera there are two possibilities for movement: movement of the camera and movement in the frame. Usually both are happening at the same time, and that's a lot to keep track of.

FIRST THINGS FIRST

OK, you've got your digital camera and you are itching to do something with it. First of all, get used to holding it. Get used to all the buttons because you'll have to find those without looking. It's useful to have something specific to accomplish while you are learning, so here are two things to try that will teach you a lot about visual storytelling and cinematography.

1 My Neighborhood: A Day in the Life

Do a visual exploration of where you live—whether it's your neighborhood, your town or city, or the fields and streams around your home. Film from morning to night. Imagine that someone who has no idea about you or where you're from wants this information in a film. You want to give a sense of how you feel about the area and what kind of place it is.

Tip: If you were telling a story with words, you'd say, "This happened, then that happened, then you'll never guess what happened next." Telling a story through film is very much like that, too. So look at what you've shot, see what is missing, and then go out and get it.

2 Playing with Genre

The word "genre" is French for "type" or "category." In film, genre refers to different kinds of movies, like horror films, action films, and comedies. You can make your movie funny or scary just by how you film it. The visuals alone and how you juxtapose them can make people laugh or be frightened.

So take your camera and go out to an event and decide what genre you want to try out.

Tip: If you want to make someone look scary, film them from a low angle (that's when the camera is way below the subject). This will make the person look large and ominous.

Film Fest

IT'S NOT JUST A FILM, IT'S A TRAVELOGUE

Neighborhoods and cities are often profiled in films.

CHRIS COLUMBUS
HOME ALONE 2: LOST IN NEW YORK

If you haven't been to Manhattan, Kevin's exploration of the city will give you a pretty thorough tour.

DAISY VON SCHERLER MAYER
MADELINE

This movie invites the viewer into various parts of Paris with friendly, warm shots of the city.

DZIGA VERTOV
MAN WITH A MOVIE CAMERA

This film documents a day in the life of a fictional city. When you watch it, you'll think you're watching the first music video ever.

CHAPTER 3

From Idea to Script

A musician begins by picking up an instrument. A dancer begins by moving to a piece of music. Where do you begin as a filmmaker?

Filmmaking usually begins with the writing of a script. The script, or screenplay, is not like a novel or a poem; it is a different form of writing very specific to film.

Anyone can shoot three minutes of video, but filmmaking is so much more than turning on the camera. Lots of decisions need to be made at the writing stage. Locations need to be described, and actors need lines. The script must also focus on what you want to see in each scene.

Stories for films are told visually, so you must learn to think and write visually. You can begin by imagining an interesting character or a place that is unique. Go to places that excite your mind, your emotions, and—very specifically—your eyes. And then practice writing down what you see and imagine clearly. Down the road, you're going to pass that sense of excitement along—first in your script, and then in your film.

It really is time to explore both the world and yourself. And like all explorers, you must be fearless.

Don't censor yourself! Being creative involves trusting your intuition. Don't worry if what you write is bad or good. All your ideas are worthwhile. Play around with those ideas and have fun.

Your film is about how you see the world. And what you write is how you want to share that experience or perspective with others. Writing can also take quite a bit of time, so be patient with yourself. It is worth taking your time. If you begin with a strong script, you are well on your way to making a strong film.

What's in a
Screenplay
?

The screenplay is the writing that gets made into the film.

There are certain elements (another word would be conventions) that appear in almost all dramatic screenplays, including setting, location, characters, dialogue, directions, and structure. These are worth knowing about ahead of writing the script so you can keep them in mind as you go along.

SETTING

This is the "where" of both the entire screenplay and each individual scene. A story has to take place somewhere. Setting takes some thought because it involves making a decision on the time period, too.

LOCATION

Location also has to do with where, but it's more specific. A scene can take place in the country or the city. Outside or inside. And if it takes place in a house, you have to specify the kitchen, a bedroom, or any other room. This is location.

CHARACTERS

The characters are the people in the story. Can you think of a film that doesn't have people in it? (There are some, but they are very rare.) The people in the film are crucial—and not just the main characters, but the supporting characters as well. As a writer, you need to think about how old a character is, where she's from, where she's living, how she dresses. Writers spend a lot of time creating characters that are believable.

DIALOGUE

In most films, people talk. Sometimes they talk a lot, and sometimes not so much. But in either case, dialogue is an essential ingredient of the screenplay.

DIRECTIONS

In films, people do things. It's the writer's job to give the characters actions, whether they are large and dramatic (like flying an airplane) or small and understated (like washing dishes while in conversation). Characters in films very rarely sit around and do nothing.

STRUCTURE

Structure is how you tell the story. For instance, you can tell a story chronologically, which means you tell it one event after another. That's a linear structure. But some movies can be told in a nonlinear way.

You could have the ending come first, for example, and then show the events that lead up to the ending.

CHECK IT OUT

Check out the next film you watch to see whether it has all these elements.

What a Script Looks Like

Most scripts include dialogue, directions, and setting.

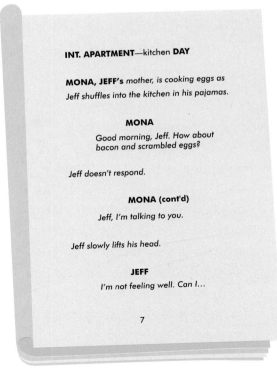

INT. APARTMENT—kitchen DAY

MONA, JEFF's mother, is cooking eggs as Jeff shuffles into the kitchen in his pajamas.

MONA
Good morning, Jeff. How about bacon and scrambled eggs?

Jeff doesn't respond.

MONA (cont'd)
Jeff, I'm talking to you.

Jeff slowly lifts his head.

JEFF
I'm not feeling well. Can I...

7

The Importance of the Script

It would be impossible to exaggerate the importance of having a strong script. There's a saying in the film industry: "You can't make a good movie from a poor script."

66 The screenplay is the basis for every film. It is where we begin when we are working on a film. So if we think of a film as a building, the script is the foundation. And in construction as in filmmaking, you must have a strong foundation. 99

—Allan A. Goldstein
SCRIPTWRITER, DIRECTOR
THE OUTSIDE CHANCE OF MAXIMILIAN GLICK

Where Films Come From

Writers often look at their own experiences to find material. They also use their imaginations to add on to that material.

When you combine life and imagination, you will usually come up with a good idea. For a good idea to be the basis of a film, it is important that you create a story from it that lends itself to visual storytelling.

THE PEOPLE IN YOUR FILM

Like good stories, memorable characters come from your life experience, your imagination, or a combination of the two. You must be both observant and creative. For example, you probably know a wealth of interesting people, either closely or just in passing. Do a character study of one of these people, making a note of their mannerisms and gestures. Later, use some of those mannerisms or gestures to make a fictional character seem more real.

Let's say that after you start basing a character on one of your friends, you realize the character needs some really out-of-the-ordinary and revealing traits. Well, that's when your imagination kicks into high gear.

HEY, GRANDMA, TELL ME ABOUT WHEN YOU WERE YOUNG

Your family history can sometimes be a great source of stories. Some of our parents, grandparents, relatives, and family friends have incredible stories to tell. Guess what? You can make your grandma's life story into a film.

NO END TO POSSIBILITIES

One thing about life: it offers an endless supply of stories. You are probably thinking about a few right now. Make a list. And beside each story idea, write some details and what you like about it. Once you have your list, live with it for a while. Your mind will slowly weed out the weaker ideas and keep the good ones. After a few days, ask yourself, "What idea am I still excited about?"

KEEP A JOURNAL

A journal is a great way to express yourself. But how will it work for you as a filmmaker or writer? Well, a journal is a place to keep all those random story ideas so you don't forget them.

Your ideas are important. Like dreams, your ideas might be indecipherable when they first come to you. But if you write them down and keep going back to them, their importance might become clear.

CONSCIOUS AND SUBCONSCIOUS

Not to get all psychological on you, but if you talk to writers, they'll usually say that ideas come to them in the following two very different ways:

1. By treating writing like a job. This means sitting down and getting to work, which in turn means writing and not worrying if what you've written is any good. If you don't have anything written, there is nothing to rewrite, and rewriting always makes writing better. That's the conscious approach to developing your ideas.

2. By always having something with you so you can write really fast, focusing only on the idea. You can create a book of your ideas, and whenever something interesting comes to you, you just write it down. It doesn't matter where you are or when it is. It doesn't matter whether the idea's good or not—you'll figure that out later. That's the subconscious approach to developing your ideas.

Writing Dialogue

An important aspect of good dialogue is that it must sound real, even though dialogue in film isn't actually real.

For instance, if two people have a disagreement in real life, it might last an hour. On film, you can't devote an hour to one scene. So the job of the scriptwriter is to cut down that hour to a couple of minutes of screen time. Nevertheless, the scene still has to feel real or natural.

ENTER LATE, LEAVE EARLY

Try to write each scene so that it takes place in as short a time as possible. That means you can't have a lot of introductory dialogue before you get to what is crucial. Have the characters say only what is important, and end the scene when that has been accomplished.

Try This: Take a recording device (your cell phone or anything that will record sound) and tape your friends or family having some ordinary conversation around the dinner table (make sure to let them know you're doing it first!). When you are finished with the recording, start writing down (transcribing) what you've recorded. This will give you an idea what real dialogue is like—it's often indirect and takes a long time to get to the point. In fact, sometimes very little is said in an hour's conversation.

This won't work in films. The challenge for the writer is to take what might in reality take an hour and distill it into two minutes. That's what we mean when we say that dialogue has to sound natural, even when it's actually not.

WE ALL HAVE AN ACCENT

How our characters speak reveals a lot about them. If a character speaks with a French accent, we might assume she is from Quebec or France. If a character uses an extensive vocabulary, we might assume that he is well educated or intelligent. So, when you are writing dialogue, it is very important that you consider where your character is from and what his or her background is.

TWO HEADS ARE SOMETIMES BETTER THAN ONE

Keeping everything organized, coming up with creative ideas, and writing an engaging and entertaining story can be a lot for one mind to keep track of. That's why many scriptwriters work in pairs. Working together can be complicated, but it can also be a lot of fun, and you may just come up with a better script than you could have written on your own. Plus, writing takes a lot of time and can be quite lonely if you do it hour after hour by yourself.

COMPROMISE AND COOPERATION

Writing with someone else can be tricky. Sometimes people don't share the same work habits. One person likes to work in the morning, the other at night. One person likes to take frequent breaks, the other prefers not to stop until it's done. Remember that differing views can make for a good script. How boring would it be to work with someone who thinks and acts exactly like you?

Film Fest

THE THINGS PEOPLE SAY

Good dialogue can come in various forms. Sometimes we remember a memorable line from a film—like short, punchy lines or long, dramatic monolgues.

MELISSA MATHISON
E.T. THE EXTRA-TERRESTRIAL

Who can forget the very short and simple "E.T., phone home"? That line contains the emotion we all feel when we're far from home and want to go back.

DAVID M. EVANS & ROBERT GUNTER
THE SANDLOT

The dialogue transports us to a rural California neighborhood in 1962, even though many of us were not alive then.

SPIKE JONZE & DAVE EGGERS
WHERE THE WILD THINGS ARE

This movie is an example of using a minimum amount of dialogue to tell a maximum amount of story.

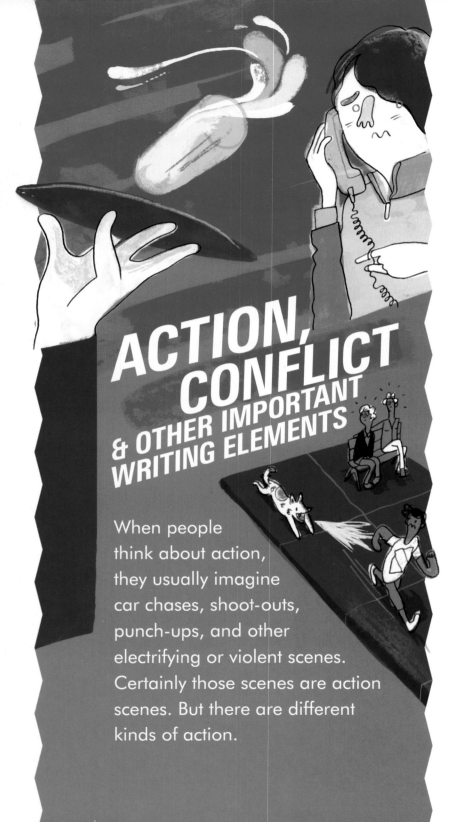

ACTION, CONFLICT
& OTHER IMPORTANT WRITING ELEMENTS

When people think about action, they usually imagine car chases, shoot-outs, punch-ups, and other electrifying or violent scenes. Certainly those scenes are action scenes. But there are different kinds of action.

CONFLICT IS DRAMA AND DRAMA IS CONFLICT

Think about some of your favorite films. Then think about the characters and stories in those films. An exciting film is about someone doing things, not sitting back and doing nothing while the world passes by. We love films that are dramatic even when they are comedies. Good drama is about people in conflict.

CONFLICT: IT ISN'T JUST ABOUT PEOPLE FIGHTING

In nearly all films, someone wants something, and there is usually an obstacle in the way. That's really the key to creating conflict. A boy might want a girl's attention, or someone might want to climb a mountain. Simply seeing the boy get the girl or seeing someone climb a mountain isn't all that interesting. However, if you place an obstacle in the way or create a problem that the character needs to overcome, you will create real drama that's interesting to write about and engaging for an audience.

RESOLUTION

In the beginning, we are introduced to the characters and the main conflict. In the middle, we see all the action that takes place. (It's actually called rising action, because the tension builds.) And in the end, the conflict is either resolved or not. That's called the resolution. That's basically how most stories work.

BUSINESS

There are also actions that aren't violent and don't lead to big action scenes. Instead, they are small actions that a character may do to show the audience what he or she is thinking, feeling, or wanting. They can be anything from cooking or eating to little idiosyncrasies like incessantly twirling hair when nervous. This is called business. Business can certainly make a character interesting, and it can also be revealing. A character in a film always has business to do.

BE SPECIFIC

This applies to where people live as well. All homes are different, so describe the one in your story clearly. Is it modern? Older? Are the furnishings expensive and new or old hand-me-downs? A lot of books? None at all? Where people live and what they choose to have around them is really important—it shows you a lot about who someone is.

APPEARANCE: WHAT CHARACTERS WEAR REVEALS A LOT

You need to know how old your characters are and what each one is wearing. A character cannot be generic. For instance, you don't want to describe someone as a teenager who is dressed "typically." For one thing, thirteen years old is very different from nineteen years old. For another, absolutely no one dresses "typically." Everyone has his or her own style, even if it resembles the style of many other people.

WRITING YOUR SHORT FILM
Some Nuts and Bolts

Here are a few tips and suggestions to help you write your script. You don't need to follow all this exactly, but it may help show you just how your ideas can come together. Scriptwriters understand the rules and conventions, but sometimes they deviate from them.

Before you begin, you need to have the following:

- your journal
- your story ideas
- all the notes and scribblings that you've been working on

Step One

Read through all the writing you've been doing. What jumps out at you as good? Are there a few story ideas you just can't get out of your mind? That's your raw material. Take those ideas and place them right in front of you.

Step Two

Decide on a main character. What does this character want most of all? It could be a thing, a person, or anything else in life.

> *Tip:* Write a character bio, which is a two- or three-page biography of your main character. This will help you make sure you know and understand him or her thoroughly.

Step Three

Create a physical setting. Where does your character live? Where is the story going to happen? In a city? In the country?

Step Four

The character has family and friends. Who are they? Are they important to the story? Figure out who is important. Which other characters will appear in the script?

Step Five

Now that you've developed a main character with an objective, think of an obstacle—that is, something seemingly insurmountable that gets in the way of your main character getting what he or she wants. The obstacle could be a person, a situation, or a flaw in your character's personality. Whatever you decide on, it needs to be so realistic that we think the main character will never ever get what he or she wants. If you do this well, you are setting up your script to have really interesting conflict and tension.

Step Six

Write out the sequence of scenes. It's a story, so think of it like this: "First this happens, then that happens, then he does this and she does that, and finally, they all do that." That's how we tell stories, and that's how scripts work, too. This is called the plot.

SHORTER IS BETTER

Almost every director began his or her career by making short films, and there are lots of good reasons for this. With short films, you can try almost anything. Millions of dollars aren't on the line, so if you make a mistake, who cares? You move on to the next one.

As we say in the industry, you earn your chops by making short films. Plus, you can have a blast doing it. (By the way, there are many film festivals for short films, so if you make a really good one, it can play all over the world.)

Film Fest

SHORT ON TIME, LONG ON ENTERTAINMENT

Short films don't receive as much publicity as features. Nevertheless, many short films are made every year. And because they are short, there is an opportunity for the filmmaker to be creative without having to invest too much time or money.

WILLIAM JOYCE & BRANDON OLDENBURG
THE FANTASTIC FLYING BOOKS OF MR. MORRIS LESSMORE

This animated short won the Academy Award in 2012. It is an amusing and emotional story that does not use any dialogue—a perfect example of showing and not telling (which we'll get to later).

DAVID CADIZ
ADVENTURES OF OWEN

This film from Humber College was voted Best Student Film in 2010 by the Toronto Film Critics Association. The story is told primarily with action.

JOHAN BRISINGER
PASSING HEARTS

Another award-winning film that's a touching story about a fourteen-year-old boy who is a heart-transplant recipient and meets the donor's parents.

Let the Rewriting Begin

Professional writers have a saying: "Writing is rewriting." When you rewrite, you are honing all the elements of your script. So don't worry if you think your rough draft isn't so good. You're now going to make it much better.

A CHECKLIST

It's easy to say rewrite and not so easy to do it, so here are some specifics to focus on.

The Characters

Have you given enough detailed description? This includes things like each character's age, physical attributes, clothing style, mannerisms, and name.

Dialogue

Is there too much or too little? Does each character have a style of speech that is reflective of their background and attitude? Does it sound natural?

Action

Does the action occur during your story, or did it all happen before your story began? If it all happens before, as part of the backstory, it could be a sign that your story needs to begin earlier.

Big Questions

• Does the story make sense? This seems obvious because it probably makes sense to you, but will it make sense to others without any explanation?

• Am I telling the story clearly and concisely?

Show, Don't Tell

"Show, don't tell" is one of the most important phrases in scriptwriting. It means that it is much better to show the audience something than simply to tell them. So if a character is happy, for instance, you want to show that happiness—by having the person burst into smiles, perhaps, and maybe dance around a bit and hug a friend. You don't want the character simply to say, "I'm happy." That's telling the audience, not showing.

We Need to See It

To make your script stronger, look for every time you use the word "feel" or "think"—then create an action for your character that shows it. For instance, if Bob finds a great job, don't just write that Bob "feels" ecstatic. Describe Bob doing something that shows how happy he is. For example, "Bob throws his hands into the air, jumps up, and dances his way into the kitchen for dinner."

MY FIRST EXPERIENCE

I'd always written things like poems and stories, but not in a very disciplined way. Depending on how I was feeling, I could write a lot in a short period of time or nothing at all for months. After I'd been acting for a few years, I wanted to write a script, but I knew the way I had always worked just wouldn't do. I decided that every day I would go to the library to work. I didn't write the whole time—sometimes I daydreamed or looked at books. But after a month, I actually had the entire first draft of my script written.

Where You Begin

Not every word a professional writes is great. But it's important to write something first and then make it better later.

> 66 I always call the first draft of a script the 'kitchen sink' draft. You throw down all your ideas and try to make sense of them. With rewriting, you start to refine and define your characters, theme, and plot. It's much like a sculptor with a piece of clay. Bit by bit, you shape it into something great. 99
>
> —Mark Achtenberg
> **SCREENWRITER, EDITOR**

Tip: Procrastination is the biggest enemy of writers. (I know—I do it all the time.) So once you are beyond the preliminary stages (such as writing ideas in a journal) and are actually working on the script, the best way to get it finished is to set aside some time every day to sit in your chair and write.

Compliments & Criticism

"Is it any good?"

We always ask ourselves this, and we do want to know. Feedback involves asking for criticisms of and compliments about your script.

Sometimes criticism is hard to receive because we always want people to love what we write. But it is crucial that we learn what is effective in our scripts and what needs more work. And since we know that writing is rewriting, it's good to receive input from people about what they think could be improved.

GUIDELINES FOR RECEIVING CRITICISM

Even the most experienced scriptwriters have problems hearing criticism. So there are some basic rules you should try to follow, or things you should try to remember, when you're receiving feedback.

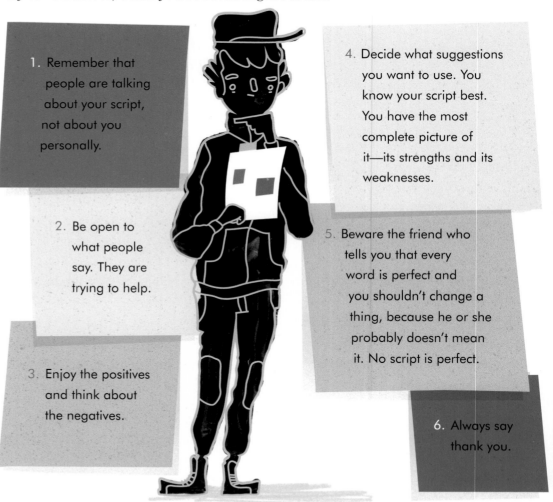

1. Remember that people are talking about your script, not about you personally.

2. Be open to what people say. They are trying to help.

3. Enjoy the positives and think about the negatives.

4. Decide what suggestions you want to use. You know your script best. You have the most complete picture of it—its strengths and its weaknesses.

5. Beware the friend who tells you that every word is perfect and you shouldn't change a thing, because he or she probably doesn't mean it. No script is perfect.

6. Always say thank you.

Every writer should cultivate readers who will always tell the truth, whether the script is good, bad, or somewhere in between. Those are the best readers to have.

TEST YOUR SCRIPT

Read the script aloud with different people taking different parts. Ask your friends to participate. They'll probably do it for the fun of it. Sit everyone around a table and give each person a role. Record the reading—it'll be useful later.

You'll get a sense of whether the story is working or still needs more rewriting. You'll get a sense of each character, each line of dialogue, and the overall structure. Identifying the strengths and weaknesses will help guide your rewriting.

IT AIN'T OVER UNTIL IT'S OVER

The script can continue to be tweaked until the day it goes before the camera. But hold on—you can't just keep writing and writing forever. So how do you know when to say, "This is it—this is what we're shooting"?

There is no scientific formula for this, but there are a few indicators:

1. No one has more suggestions on how to make it better.
2. You have a gut feeling that the story is working: it has a beginning, a middle, and an end that you are happy with.
3. You have given yourself a deadline and that deadline is now.

Will I *Ever* Be Finished?

Knowing when a script is finished is difficult. Scriptwriters tend to continue to write until they can't anymore.

> **"**I don't think you're ever finished writing a film until you're finished the movie. I've worked in both film and television, and I have made a couple of shorts of my own. You are tweaking until the end. **"**
>
> —Katrina Saville
> **WRITER, DIRECTOR, SCRIPT SUPERVISOR**

The Storyboard
The Script Comes to Life

What is a storyboard? Basically, it's a group of sketches of what the film will look like when it is shot.

"BUT I CAN'T DRAW!"

Even if you can't draw, the storyboard is key. If you are a fine drawer, that's great. If not, use stick figures. Technically, what you are doing is breaking down the action of the script into shots, and that's exactly what they do on the big Hollywood movies, too. The storyboard gives everyone a first peek at what the film will look like. It's like the architectural blueprint for a building.

1. Your storyboard sketches could look like this:

2. But don't worry if you can't draw that well. It's fine for them to look like this:

TIME TO BE CREATIVE AND HAVE FUN

The storyboard is like the script—it can go through many drafts. For many filmmakers, this is the most exciting time. You are beginning to visualize what your film will look like. Try anything that comes to mind as a visual idea. That's how film directors come up with unique ideas—they let their imaginations run wild.

44

IT'S A MOVIE!

Once you are happy with your storyboard, there are a few more things you can do to prepare for filming.

1. Take a camera and film each frame of the storyboard for at least ten seconds.

2. Take the sound recording you made of your friends reading the script.

3. Input both the recording and the pictures of the storyboard into your computer.

4. Edit the sound to the storyboard. It doesn't need to be fancy. Just figure out what dialogue goes with what image and edit them together. You can do this on a very basic editing program.

When this is done, guess what? You now have your very first draft of the film, which is totally exciting.

The Joys of Storyboard

Storyboards are much more than just pretty pictures.

66 Drawing a storyboard is like making a film. You have to think of camera placement and movement, composition, and how the action will be choreographed—you even have to think of the actors' performances. And always you are working from the script and telling the story visually as best you can. 99

—Eric Cator
STORYBOARD ARTIST, EDITOR

Try This: Take a scene from one of your favorite movies. Break the scene down into its individual components (the shots). List each shot, and then draw a storyboard based on the scene. It's a way to learn how to storyboard and to understand how the pros actually construct a scene. For example, if you like action movies, take a really intense action scene and do the storyboard for that. You'll learn how to film action and anything else you're interested in.

CHAPTER 4

Lights, Camera, Action

You've got the script—and it's a good one—and you are really charged because you know that you could have a super movie on your hands if it's just done well. So how can you make that happen? It's time to find yourself a crew and a cast.

A good film is magical. But one magician doesn't make a film. All movies take a lot of work by a lot of people. And they are made all over the world. Like technology, like music, and like fashion, the film business is a massive industry employing lots of people. One thing those people have in common is that at some point they probably said, "Hey, this is what I want to do."

Making a film is like living and working in a small village. Everybody is related and interdependent. This means that each person needs every other person. In a village, there is the mayor, the baker, the grocer, the firefighter, the police officer, the teacher, the car dealer, the banker, etc. On a film set, there is the director, the actors, the cinematographer, the sound recordist, the props person, the makeup artist, and so many more.

And everyone needs to be connected. The sound recordist needs to know what the cinematographer is doing. The cinematographer works closely with the actors. The actors take their lead from the director. They must all work as one, but at the same time, each individual must do his or her own job very well.

So the idea is to create your village. Find friends who share your passion. You can't do it alone. It's all about collaboration—working together.

GETTING ORGANIZED

How do you get everyone in the right place at the right time? How do you know what to do first? And what and when are the cast and crew going to eat? Making a film demands organization.

SCRIPT BREAKDOWN

Well, on a professional set, a production manager would do what we call a script breakdown, but on your film, you will probably be doing the breakdown yourself. And just what is a script breakdown? You are going to go through the script multiple times and do the following:

· List the characters by name, gender, and age.

· List the locations and note whether each one is an interior (indoors) or an exterior (outdoors).

· List any specific props that characters need to have on set. For instance, if a character walks around with a guitar, list that. If two characters have tea together, list those items.

· Count the number of shots in every scene. You can do this by consulting the storyboard.

· Count the number of scenes that happen during the day and the number that happen at night.

THE PRODUCTION BINDER

You are now beginning to create something that will be very important to your film: a production binder. What goes in the production binder? The script, the storyboard, the script breakdown, the budget, and your notes about absolutely everything.

THE CALL SHEET

How do you get everyone in one place at the right time? You put together something called the call sheet.

What is a call sheet? Well, it's a document that has all the information about where you are filming, who is supposed to be there and at what time, when everyone will finish, when and where lunch is, and anything else important. People don't show up magically at the right location. They need the information.

SCHEDULING BASICS

How do you know when to film? If you are shooting interiors, the answer is simple: you film whenever it's convenient. When you are shooting exteriors, you must consider when it's convenient for cast and crew, what time of day the script calls for, and when you can secure the location.

"AAARGH! STUFF COSTS MONEY!"

That's true, but no need to sweat; your first film isn't going to cost millions. Or thousands. And maybe not even hundreds. Why? Because you are resourceful and prudent, you're not going to pay anyone, and you're going to ask for lots and lots of favors.

MAKE A BUDGET

The film will cost you something—that's unavoidable—so it's good to understand that and then give yourself a budget that's realistic.

FOOD

Even if nothing else costs, plan on spending some money on food so that your cast and crew know you appreciate them. Once you've cajoled your friends and family into coming to your set at 7 a.m. because you need a large group of people for that beautiful sunrise shot, you'd better have some goodies for them to eat.

WHAT DOES A BUDGET LOOK LIKE?

First figure out how much money you have. Then figure out what you need to spend money on and how much you need to spend on each thing.

JUGGLING THE PENNIES

Sometimes you need more money for a costume, let's say, so you take it from another budget item. Budgeting is an important part of producing, and like everything else in film, it is creative.

Getting It
DONE

You are the director. Whoopee! Wait, what is a director? Well, the director is the person who says, "Lights, camera, action." And does so much more.

Most important, the director is a visual storyteller. That's the main part of the job description. But as the director, at different times you're going to be one or more of the following:

· a leader

· a manager

· a psychologist

· an acting coach

· a disciplinarian

· and a shining example of how to work on a film

8 SIMPLE RULES
FOR EVERYONE WORKING ON YOUR FILM

1. Never be late.

2. Always be pleasant.

3. Do your own job well.

4. Look for ways to help others do their jobs well.

5. Don't leave the set without telling someone and making sure it's OK.

6. Talk quietly at all times.

7. Be silent when the actors are working their scenes.

8. At the end of the day, say good-bye to everyone and make sure everything that needs to be done has been done.

AND DON'T FORGET

You, as the director, model good working habits by adhering to these simple rules at all times. If you do this, everyone else will follow suit.

Tip: Do you want to be a director? Before you make your film, try to get as much experience as possible working with actors. And to really understand what an actor has to deal with, try being one yourself. Get in front of a camera. Don't just goof around—try acting out a role. That's one of the best ways to learn about directing actors.

A First Time Directing

Every director has to direct for the first time. And it isn't easy having a lot of people looking to you for answers to everything.

66 The first time on set, there is a bit of nervousness and excitement. It's important to have faith and trust in your crew, and that cuts down the anxiety a bit. It's the calm before the storm, and it's good to take a breath, be confident in what you need to do, and be prepared for the unexpected. 99

—David Cadiz
WRITER, DIRECTOR, VISUAL EFFECTS

The Crew
Working with Friends, Relatives & Strangers

When you don't have money, whom do you end up working with? Your family and friends, of course.

Because they will help you out. But working with people close to you can be tricky because you're not just hanging out. You actually have to accomplish things—a lot of things. There are all kinds of demands on you, and you are going to make all kinds of demands of those around you.

SOME GROUND RULES

· Tell people exactly what's involved (starting sometimes at 5 a.m., no money, outdoor shoot in the rain, etc.).

· Never guilt someone into working with you. If someone has to be convinced, it's going to end up being a problem.

· Act like a professional even though you're not one.

· Move on if someone doesn't want to do something for you. An enthusiastic participant will always do a better job.

WHERE TO SHOOT

One way to simplify things is to shoot in your family's apartment or house. This means a big favor from your family, but it's one well worth trying to get. You'll save on travel time and money, and it also means you don't have to go looking for locations like a kitchen, a bedroom, and a basement.

Tip: If it doesn't affect the story, change the locations to suit what is easiest for you to find. You might want a penthouse apartment, but if a family member's bedroom will do the trick, use it.

SHOOTING ON LOCATION

The first rule of shooting on location—whether it's in your house or someone else's—is to leave it in better shape than you found it. Sometimes you have to move furniture around, bring in food, and do other things. But when you leave, the place should be spotless. Why? For two main reasons: first, it's the professional thing to do, and second, if you ever want to film there again, you'll hear, "Sure, you left the place so clean last time."

In the movie business, when people abuse somewhere they are filming, it's called burning a location. It means that no one can ever film there again.

Film Fest

FILMS ABOUT MAKING FILMS

The following films are very different from one another. But each one is about the making of films.

MICHEL GONDRY
BE KIND REWIND

This is a wacky movie about two clerks in a video store who accidentally erase a lot of movies. They then try to reshoot those movies to replace them.

GENE KELLY & STANLEY DONEN
SINGIN' IN THE RAIN

This is one of the most popular movies of all time, and it has Hollywood and filmmaking as its backdrop. You learn a lot about what goes on behind the scenes from this movie.

PETER CRAIG
THE CLIMACTIC DEATH OF DARK NINJA

This short movie is about a group of students trying to shoot the last scene of their film. It portrays the passion and humor of making movies.

The Talent

Good acting can bring the quality of your production way up. Poor acting can make your life miserable and frustrating.

A huge part of being the director is working with actors. It's also a huge part of the fun of being a director.

WORKING WITH THE TALENT

So how do you work with actors? By communicating with them, trusting them, and giving them feedback during rehearsal and on set.

How do you give actors feedback? Be specific—don't generalize. The words "good" or "bad" used without any more direct reference to what was good or bad can be confusing. In fact, rather than using a weighted word like "good," try saying, "That really worked for me because I felt the emotion of the moment much more strongly that time." Then the actor knows exactly what was good.

"LET'S DO IT AGAIN, AND AGAIN"

Rehearsals are an integral part of the creative process of developing a film. They are a chance to get to know your actors, to see how each of them works, and to learn what kind of direction will be helpful. You'll be able to see how the script is working and whether the drama or comedy of each scene is as clear and effective as it could be.

Rehearsals are also an opportunity for you to do rewrites. Really good actors can give you some great ideas. You don't have to take their ideas (use only what you feel will make the film better, just as you would with anyone else who gives you feedback). But who better than the person playing the role to tell you about the character?

RUNNING A REHEARSAL

Make sure that you meet at a predetermined time, and that everyone knows when the rehearsal will be finished.

1. Start with a table read. This is when all the actors sit around a table and read the script line by line. This is the time for the actors to ask you any questions they have about the characters, specific lines of dialogue, or anything else that comes to mind.

2. Have the actors get on their feet and, one scene at a time, begin acting the lines while moving in whatever way feels natural to them. After each scene, give each actor feedback and a specific direction.

3. Now go through each scene again, showing the actors where you hope to have the camera and where you are planning to place them as you shoot the scene. This is called blocking the actors for camera.

4. Get feedback from the actors. If something doesn't feel right to someone, see if you can change it, and answer any more questions your actors have at this point.

5. End the rehearsal on a positive note. Say something like, "You were all great. I know you're going to make this story come alive."

6. Most important, make any necessary changes to the script or the blocking. You will only be making your film better and better.

The Dangers of Stereotypes in Casting

The casting process—when you choose your actors—is crucial to a film's success. It's important to see beyond what actors look like (how much they might look like how you envisioned characters) and focus on their talent (how well they can portray characters).

66 The casting process really works well if the filmmaker understands that it is always best to cast the strongest actor. You may visualize your character as a tall blonde, but if the shorter brunette is the best actor, cast her. In fact, good casting sees beyond race, age, gender, and physical appearances. 99

—Ashley Bowes
CASTING DIRECTOR

The Shoot Begins!

This is the busiest you'll ever be. It's a lot of work...and a lot of fun. But you must be prepared. Two items from the production binder that you need to have on set are the storyboard and the shot list. The shot list is a catalog of the shots you need to do and the order in which you're going to do them. You need to be able to communicate these things to your crew members so they can be prepared. You might have everything in your head, but make sure you also have it on paper.

Camera Department
Is the camera placement correct? How about the lighting and the composition?

Art Department
Does everything look right? Is the set decorated properly? What about costumes and hair?

Script
Are the lines totally right? Does anything need changing?

Sound Department
Are the actors' lines being recorded clearly?

Talent
Are we getting the absolute best performances from the actors?

Assistant Director
Is everything organized properly? Will we get all the shots today and finish on time?

Entire Crew
Am I setting a tone on set that is pleasant, fun, and conducive to efficient work?

56

FOUR GOLDEN RULES FOR YOU

1. Don't get stressed out.
   Keep your cool. No screaming!

2. Be creative.

3. Solve any problems that arise.
   You have it in you to do it.

4. Have a blast! (Why would you ever
   want to do this if it's not fun?)

THE FIRST SHOT

Whether it's the first shot of the entire shoot or the first of the day, you always want to make it a good one because it will set the tone for what follows. So choose something that isn't too demanding technically and isn't overly emotional for the actors. That way, the day will begin with a success.

Tip: Even if you have only a small crew, try to have someone on set whose job is to watch continuity. This person is called the script supervisor. It's important that everything in a film look right. So if a cup is full in one shot, it must be full in the next shot as well. When continuity isn't right, things look silly, and that distracts viewers from the story.

GIVE FEEDBACK

After each shot, let the actors know what worked for you and what didn't. And don't forget about the technical crew (especially the camera operator)! Try saying something like, "That looked great, but let's do it again and try to time the pan closer to the actor when he moves."

You always want both cast and crew to feel positive and to build on their strengths.

DECISIONS, DECISIONS, DECISIONS

It sometimes seems that filmmaking is a never-ending series of decisions. For everything that is done on a film, there are always at least two ways of doing it. (Actually, there are usually hundreds of ways of doing anything on a film!) So everyone is always trying to make the best decision given the situation.

Relationships Are So Important

A director needs a lot of know-how and a vision. What sometimes is forgotten is the importance of relationships.

66 When I first get to set I start by sincerely thanking all the cast and crew, in a group setting as well as one on one, for being part of the project. It's important for me that they know how much I value their input. A crew must respect the director's vision, and to get that respect you have to give it. With mutual respect, things always work out. 99

—Mazi Khalighi
DIRECTOR, *FOREIGN SOIL*

On the
PROFESSIONAL FILM SET

It might be quite a while before you are working with the pros, but it's still worth taking a look at what a professional set looks like.

(1) The actors are the focus of attention. The action happens all around them.

(2) The director is never far from the epicenter. A director has to be in touch with all the key members of all departments, while also maintaining close contact with the actors.

(3) The camera captures the action. A director of photography checks the lighting, and a camera operator, well, operates the camera.

(4) The boom operator records the sound through the microphone for the sound recordist.

(5) A few people keep the actors looking good and consistent throughout the production. They take care of makeup, costume, and hair.

(6) Other people design the sets. Once you're filming, they maintain the look of each set. They are the production designer, the props person, and the set decorator.

(7) The assistant director keeps the production moving and its elements coordinated. If things slow down, it's up to the assistant director to get them back on track.

8   The cast and crew often work long hours between meals. Craft services is a place where they can have drinks and snacks at any time.

9   There is always lots and lots of equipment. Lights are everywhere—you can't film without them. There are sound blankets to make sure the quality of sound is what the director wants. And on this particular set, there is a smoke machine so that there is a feeling of fogginess.

FINISHING THE SHOOT
It's in the Can!

OK, you and your cast and crew have just been through the most exhausting and the most rewarding few days of your life. You think you have your film. You hope you have your film. Now it's time for...

THE WRAP PARTY

It's time for the celebration called the wrap party. That means you've wrapped up this part of the production, and you can take a moment to pat each other on the back. This is very important because it is your chance to relax, talk about how things went, and say thank you to all those who helped you.

What are the ingredients for a great wrap party? Good food + good music + good atmosphere = lots of fun and a happy group of people who will be tickled to be aboard the next film you make.

A BIG THANKS TO EVERYONE

This is the time to buy or make cards and write personal notes that reflect the work each person did. Yes, it's a big job that will keep you up all night, but it will be tremendously meaningful for everyone involved, including you. This is an act of thoughtfulness that pays large dividends. Each person who worked on your film will feel appreciated. That's something money just can't buy.

MAKING FILMS IS ABOUT CREATING A COMMUNITY OF FRIENDS

Friends work on your films and you work on theirs. That means you should keep your relationships positive. If you do that, the next time you make a film, everyone will want to help you because

1. You make good films;

2. The experience is enjoyable; and

3. People know how appreciative you are.

These things pay off big time as you travel down the road of filmmaking.

HEY, IF THESE BUDDIES CAN DO IT...

Once people find others they like to work with, the relationships often continue for many years. Here are a few well-known Hollywood examples of successful collaborators:

· Judd Apatow (director),
  Seth Rogen (actor),
  and Evan Goldberg (screenwriter)

· Tim Burton (director),
  Johnny Depp (actor),
  and Helena Bonham Carter (actor)

· Martin Scorsese (director)
  and Thelma Schoonmaker (editor)

· Alfred Hitchcock (director)
  and Edith Head (costume designer)

The list goes on and on.

MY EXPERIENCE: MY FRIENDS AND I ALWAYS WORK TOGETHER

A lot of the time when you're making a film, you wake up early to work a really long day. This is when you want to be working with pleasant people who are fun and get the job done. I've produced and directed over 150 shows (films and television, dramas and documentaries), and I've worked with a lot of people, but I prefer to have the same key people (director of photography, sound recordist, and editor) with me as often as possible. They are my buddies, and they make filmmaking thoroughly enjoyable. I rarely have to work with anyone but my friends, so I know that every work situation will be a good one.

CHAPTER 5

Postproduction

OK, the film is shot. You have all the footage. Now what happens?

The next phase of filmmaking is called postproduction. This includes everything that happens after the shooting has stopped, up until the film is completely finished.

There's a saying in filmmaking: "Don't worry about it. We'll fix it in post." It usually means, "We made a mistake while filming, and we'll ignore it for now in the hope that the editing will cover it up." To some degree, it is possible to fix things in postproduction. If there is a color that needs correcting, that can be done. Or if a line has been flubbed, it can often be re-recorded. But really,

it's best to do things right the first time so that people can focus on making the film even better through the editing and other processes of postproduction.

Postproduction is a creative time to make the good things even better. As the director, you will be working with another creative person: the editor. Some ideas will come from you, others from the editor, and still others from people to whom you show your film-in-progress.

In postproduction, we work with the following main elements: visuals, sounds, and special effects.

Everything that has been filmed is edited together to make scenes, and eventually those scenes are constructed into the entire movie. Existing sounds are edited, new sounds and sound effects are created, dialogue is recreated, the music is added, and it's all mixed together to make the soundtrack. Each individual sound is set so that the audience will hear exactly what the director wants them to hear at the proper volume and in sync with the right visual. If you're going to use any of those cool computer-generated effects, this is where you'd add those too.

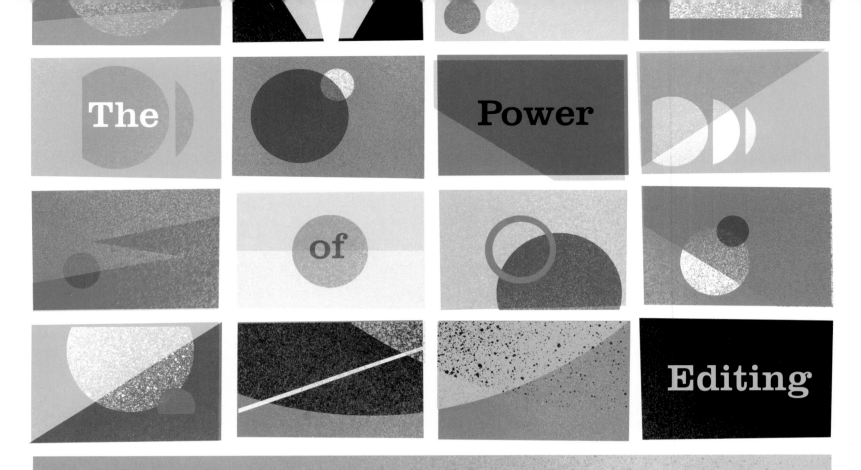

The Power of Editing

A lot of postproduction revolves around editing both the picture and the sound.

There is a lot of different digital editing software; some is pretty easy to operate, and the rest is very complicated. But editing isn't just technical—it's also creative. Editing is about rhythm, pacing, and storytelling. It's about getting the most out of the emotion of the moment and moving the story forward. It's about exploring all the possibilities created by the story and the characters.

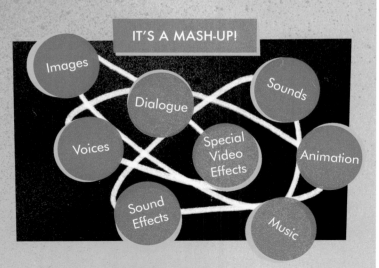

IT'S A MASH-UP!

Images
Dialogue
Sounds
Voices
Special Video Effects
Animation
Sound Effects
Music

1 + 1 = 3

When it comes to editing, one plus one does not always add up to two. One image placed next to another image can sometimes be a lot more powerful than the two separate images. That's how important editing is.

And then, when you place images next to each other—in a sequence—you have a story.

To understand what I mean, think about the following five separate images:

- a pretty flower
- a hand picking the flower
- a person looking out a window
- a person's eyes
- a door opening and someone running out

Individually, these five images don't say very much, but when they are placed in a sequence—when they are edited together—they begin to tell a story.

a. We see a very pretty flower.

b. A person is looking at it.

c. A hand goes out to pick it.

d. Someone else sees this from a window.

e. A door flies open and that person runs out toward the person picking the flower.

Now we have an active character and some drama. In other words, we have a story. If the same five images were rearranged, we would have an entirely different story.

Let's take three images from a Santa Claus parade. Place them first in one order and then another.

The same images in reverse order give a completely different meaning.

That's the power of editing.

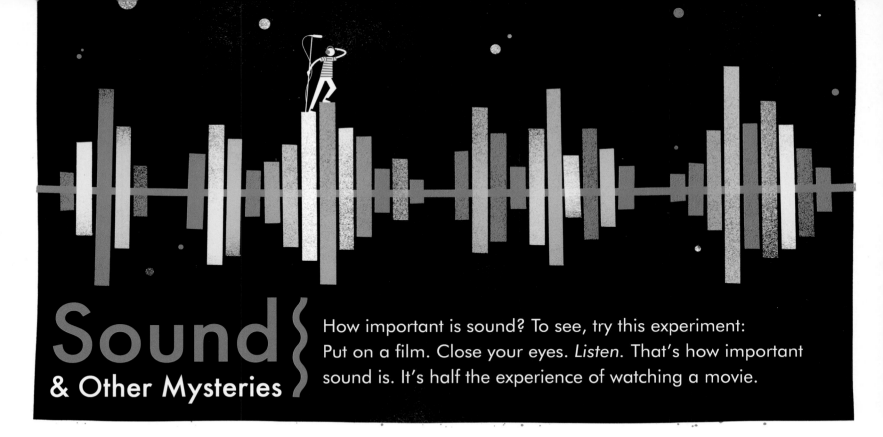

Sound
& Other Mysteries

How important is sound? To see, try this experiment: Put on a film. Close your eyes. *Listen.* That's how important sound is. It's half the experience of watching a movie.

IT'S NOT JUST PEOPLE TALKING

The sound edit is all about recreating how we actually hear various sounds.

There are a lot of elements that go into the sound of any film: the dialogue, the music, the sound effects, and much more. The sound edit is one of the most complex processes of filmmaking. I thought I'd get the step-by-step lowdown on it from Katie Halliday, a professional sound editor. Here's what she had to say:

STEP ONE
Sound Design

Many screenwriters and directors use sound as a storytelling tool. After the film is shot and the picture editor has finished editing, it's up to postproduction sound to tie it all together. Some films need totally naturalistic sound. Some directors want lots of music. Some films have background sounds that have an effect on the subconscious. All this and more goes into the overall sound design of any film.

STEP TWO
Dialogue

The sound editor now ensures that all the dialogue is clear and clean.

66

STEP THREE
ADR, or Automated Dialogue Replacement

Sometimes what is recorded on set is not usable. For example, if a film is being shot near a city, the sound of airplanes could be an unwanted intrusion. Even indoors, something like a building's air conditioning could drown out the dialogue. In these cases, parts of a performance might need to be redone by the actor using ADR. The actor would have to come to a sound studio and—while watching herself say the line that wasn't usable—repeat the line in sync with her own moving lips. In many films, the dialogue is actually all recorded separately. That way, the voices can sound exactly how the director wants (like in an animated film, where actors say the words as they watch their animated characters).

STEP FOUR
Sound Effects

Sound effects editors do a wide range of tasks, including fabricating creative sounds, like monster growls, fictional machines, and so on.

STEP FIVE
Foley

Foley is the process of recreating the everyday sounds that could not be recorded at the time of filming. Foley is subtle—it is recreating literally any sound made by any character in any shot of a film. Footsteps, clothes swishing, hands touching and moving things—these are all Foley sounds.

STEP SIX
The Mixer

The final step of postproduction sound lies with the mixer. This person must have very good hearing and judgment because, along with the director, the mixer decides on the final sound levels. I once heard someone compare a mixer to a chef who picks out all sorts of ingredients (sounds) to add to the dish (the film). Like a chef, the mixer takes all those ingredients and shapes them so they work in harmony, tasting along the way to see if anything needs to be added or removed to compose the final dish.

Film Fest
FOR YOUR EARS

The following films have evocative sound design, soundtracks, and music that transport us into the world and emotion of the film.

MARTIN SCORSESE
HUGO

This film uses sound as a storytelling tool. We often know the whereabouts of the police officer and his dog before we see them because of sound. *Hugo* shows how sound can be unrealistic yet extremely effective.

STEVEN SPIELBERG
JURASSIC PARK

This film clearly identifies the bad guys—the dinosaurs—with sound and music. In fact, in every film Spielberg makes, sound is used creatively and powerfully.

JAMES BOBIN
THE MUPPETS

This film subtly creates a puppet world with sounds and voices that are a bit different from those in the real world. It does this with inventive use of sound effects and Foley.

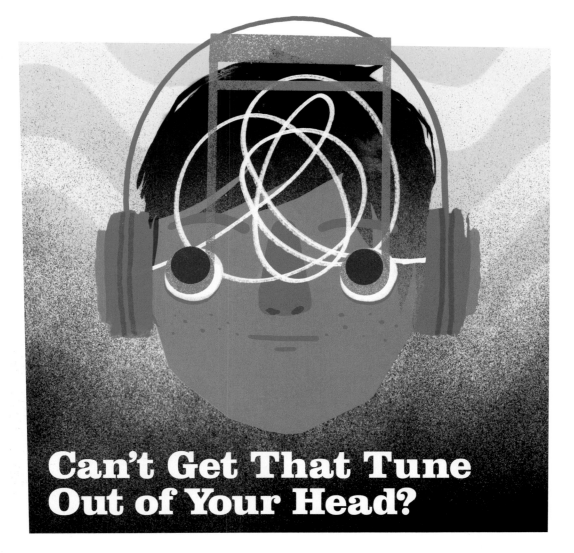

Can't Get That Tune Out of Your Head?

Music is important. It's not just in the background of a film—it's a creative element that adds a lot to the film's story. This is what music can do:

- It brings all the elements of the film together.
- It lets us know what is happening and what is going to happen.
- It can take us to a place that goes way beyond the images we view or the dialogue we hear.

"IT'S GETTING CLOSER!"

In horror films, we often know who and where the monster is because the music tells us.

Jaws is a famous example of how music can work to ratchet up the tension. The scene is iconic. It's summertime, it's hot, and the beach is crowded. People are happily swimming in the ocean. But we hear a certain melody—the melody associated with the people-eating shark—and we know something bad is about to happen. We want to scream at the swimmers, "Get out of the water!"

MUSIC IS ENERGY AND EMOTION

Don't underestimate the power of music to enhance a scene, a moment, or a character. On the other hand, don't underestimate the power of inappropriate music to deaden a crucial scene in your film! Choose wisely.

> **Tip:** Don't overpower the audience. Sometimes people don't even notice the music. That's because it is creating or enhancing the mood and atmosphere. It works with the film; it doesn't take it over.

A FEW NOTES AND YOU'RE THERE

What do you think of when you hear a banjo, a set of bagpipes, or four bars of electronic music? In an instant, with just a few bars of music, you can be carried to a specific country or time period.

SILENCE CAN BE GOLDEN

It isn't done very often, but some movies have no music (or next to none). Just as music can take you far away, having no music can have the same effect. The film *2001: A Space Odyssey* has fabulous classical music for part of it, but then there are long periods of time when it is virtually silent. The lack of music forces the audience to experience the sound qualities of outer space and the visual elements more deeply.

DON'T FORGET ABOUT COPYRIGHT

There are two ways to go about getting music for your film. One is to use existing music that you like. That's all right if you're just going to screen your film for friends, but unless you have permission, you can't screen your film in public or at film festivals. You need permission to use a piece of pre-recorded music— usually it will cost money to get this permission. An alternative is to write your own music or find a friend's band who wants to score the film for you. Hey, this could be the beginning of a fun relationship, like the one between director Steven Spielberg and composer John Williams, who have worked together on over thirty films.

Becoming a Film Composer

Writing music for films isn't simply about writing great music. A song has to work with the story the film is trying to tell, not just on its own.

> 66 I love how film challenges you to go to places in your mind you wouldn't normally go to. The music can bring feelings of tenderness, dread, tension, action, or humor to a film, and it adds another emotional level to what is happening on the screen. To do this is a serious challenge for any musician. 99

—Larry Cohen
COMPOSER

Putting It All
TOGETHER

The leading lady is running from an animated character. Spaceships are in the sky. And the hero snags a bullet from the air with his teeth. *What is going on?*

Computer-generated visual effects (VFX) can be an important component of a film. They are usually created during postproduction using various kinds of animation software. Almost anything you can imagine can be accomplished using VFX. If you're interested, it's worth taking the time to learn some elementary software. Find a friend who knows a software program or two and is willing to spend the time helping you out. Even if it's just used for your credit sequence, VFX is something that will visually wow the audience.

A WORD OF WARNING

Visual effects are expensive and time-consuming, so don't count on having them. In the scriptwriting phase, don't include a lot of effects that need to be done. It will make your filmmaking life very difficult if you base a lot of your film on having complicated special effects. Audiences won't even notice the lack of VFX as long as the story isn't lacking.

THE SOUND MIX: IT'S LIKE A STEW

In a tasty dish, you need to balance sweet and spicy, various herbs, and the strengths of the different ingredients—in much the same way, the sound mix has to balance the various elements that go into it, including dialogue, background sounds, sound effects, and music. Typically, you do an initial mix and sit with it for a while—maybe a week or two—until you get a sense of what needs to be tweaked. This is called the temp mix. When you are clear about what needs to be altered, you do the final mix. Now the work on the sound is all done.

THE CREDITS

All those who worked on the film must have their names on the screen long enough that they and everyone else can read them. Same goes for those who helped out in even the smallest way. Your mother who baked a cake for the crew. Your neighbor who moved his old car off the street so it wouldn't be in the shot. The corner grocer who let you do a close-up of a head of lettuce in his store. They all need to see their names in the credits. That's the tradition—they each receive a credit.

IS MY FILM EVER GOING TO BE FINISHED?

You've got what you think is a finished film (or at least a just-about-finished film), but you're wondering if people will understand the ending.

Or you've made a comedy, but you really need to know which jokes are funny and which ones need a bit more editing to make the punch lines work. (After you've seen a joke about a hundred times, it's hard to decide if it's funny or not.) So what do you do? You put together an audience and have a test screening. That's what the professionals do, and it's a good idea for you to do it as well.

AUDIENCES CHANGE EVERYTHING

It's an entirely different experience watching your film with maybe thirty people who are seeing it for the first time. You can learn a lot from their reactions, so make sure you are sitting in the audience and have a notebook handy. Some things will jump right out at you, and you'll ask yourself, "What was I thinking?"

A QUICK SURVEY

Create a short form for each audience member to fill out. It can include any or all of the following questions:

- What were the strongest parts of the film?
- What were the weakest parts?
- Was there enough drama?
- Was there enough comedy?
- Can you remember the funniest moment?
- Was there anything that really didn't make sense?
- Do you have any concrete suggestions for changes?
- Were there any scenes that dragged for you?
- How would you describe this film to your friends?

And don't forget to add: *Thanks for taking the time to fill out this form. We really appreciate your feedback.*

USE THIS FEEDBACK TO GUIDE YOU

You don't have to use every suggestion made in a test screening, but if most people tell you that one specific joke is really funny, you know for sure it is. And if a lot of people write that a certain scene dragged, you know it did and will need to be fixed by re-editing. It's actually exciting doing a test screening. And extremely useful. That's why they do this for the big movies, too.

THE END

That's what it feels like. It's finished. Done. Finito. Fin. And you actually have something to show for all your hard work. It's called a film. You have made a film! Congratulations!

Finishing a First Film

Making a film is a bit like running a marathon. It's exhausting and, in the end, tremendously gratifying.

" One day, you wake up from your workaholic daze to find yourself sitting in a theater watching the film that's been rolling around inside your head. Watching a film just like everyone around you. Except the film is yours. It's the most surreal, terrifying, exhilarating, transformative experience. It's your first film! "

—Michelle Latimer
DIRECTOR, WRITER

CHAPTER 6

Getting It Out There

When you make a film, you want people to see it. A film isn't something you spend months making, only to leave it in your closet.

You want to share your vision, your ideas, and most important, your story. Filmmakers want people to see what they have created. It's not about ego—it's about creating something worthwhile and sharing it. Can you imagine making up spectacular recipes and never cooking them for anyone? What a waste, right?

So who is your audience? If you made a goofy comedy, you're not going to expect your parents and all their friends to want to see it. (Well, your family will probably want to see anything you do!) You know who your audience is: people like you. You need to get it out there so they can see it. Otherwise, you may have made a gem that never shines in the light of day. And what fun would that be?

Your work is good, and people should know about it. Your marketing and publicity materials will tell them why they should see your film, buy it, or program it into a festival. People won't know about you or your film unless you tell them about it. So that's what you are going to do.

Every film you create is a step toward the next one. So even if you aren't expecting to make money on this film, you do still want people to see it and enjoy it so they'll be supportive of you when you make your next film. That's what the marketing and publicity will help you accomplish.

DIY MARKETING &PUBLICITY

You need to create materials to tell the world about your film and get people excited to see it. Big-budget films have publicists and a marketing department. But you are going DIY.

STEP ONE
Find the Perfect Still Photograph

Make sure someone is taking some really great stills of the cast on set. Find a couple of stills that really give a sense of what the film is about. You'll be using them a lot in the marketing materials.

STEP TWO
Make a Trailer

You can do this while the editing is going on. It's important to tantalize a viewer with a quick synopsis of your film. Making great trailers, or previews, is an art. (Turn the page for more on this!)

STEP THREE
Create the Poster, the One-Sheet, and the DVD Cover

These are the basic publicity materials. All three items (the one-sheet is one page of information about the film and an image) have the same information but in a different form. You want an image or two that attracts people to your film and makes them say, "Wow, that looks cool! I want to see that." You want to tell potential viewers what your film is about, so they'll think, "Great. It's a comedy. I love comedies." And you want to show them that other people have seen your film already and love it. To accomplish this last one, entice them with some quotes like, "Funny, funny film!" Or, "I laughed 'til I cried."

76

LIFE WAS SIMPLE
UNTIL IT WAS COMPLICATED

A GREAT MOVIE WITH COMEDY, TRAGEDY, AND ACTION, FEATURING AN UNKNOWN ACTOR WHO'S GOING TO BE A BIG STAR

DIRECTED BY: YOU! · STARRING:
Your grandmother · Your phys ed teacher
SPECIAL GUEST APPEARANCE BY
Your neighbor's poodle

★★★★★
"A FABULOUS FILM..."
—Your mother

★★★★
"HILARIOUS!"
—Your cousin Bill

★★★★
EST FIRST MOVIE EVER..."

STEP FOUR
Prepare the EPK

An EPK is an electronic press kit. Twenty years ago, films made physical press kits to hand out to newspapers and television stations. These days, press kits are on disc or downloadable from websites. They contain the same information as physical press kits did, including production stills, your contact information, and a bio that explains who you are. You will also want to include the credit list and the story of how the production came together. When you have everything, you can load it onto a disc and send it out to whomever you think you should.

STEP FIVE
Make Lots of Copies of Your Film to Send to People

NOT AGAIN? YES AGAIN! $!

Publicity costs. It doesn't have to cost very much, as you will see, but getting things done is easier if you have a few dollars.

"IS IT FINISHED YET?"

Naturally, everyone who contributed to the film wants to see the finished product. You've probably been telling them for months now: "It's not finished...Just a little while longer...I'll let you know." Well, now it is finished, so you need to screen it. Arrange a time and a place and send out the invitations.

Screenings are important, so make sure you have the best possible conditions: the best projection, the best sound, and the most comfortable seating. You want people to see your film the way you made it to be seen— with no apologies necessary.

MAKE YOUR TRAILER

Creating a useful trailer takes skill. It is a challenge to be creative in a limited amount of time while simultaneously stirring the audience's interest without giving away too much of the plot. The trailer must make the viewer want to see the entire film. So you want to offer a taste of it—a really pleasant taste—that leaves people curious and eager to see all of what they're missing.

IT TAKES TIME

Say it takes a month to edit a ten-minute film. Would you think that making a one-minute trailer takes one-tenth of a month? It doesn't. Making a one-minute trailer actually takes a lot of time—almost as much time as editing the entire film. That's because the trailer, which serves the important purpose of "selling" your film, must be very precise. ("Selling" in this case means tantalizing people to want to see more.)

TAKE IT TO THE MAX

If your film is suspenseful, have us feel the suspense in the trailer. If it's a drama, show us a fantastic moment between your actors. And if it's a comedy, make sure something in the trailer is a side-splitting laugh.

WHY WOULD ANYONE WANT TO WATCH THIS STORY?

It's up to you to create a trailer that shows people why they want to see your film, and a voice-over can help with that. A voice-over can also tie loose ends together, because you have so little time to do that visually.

WATCH OTHER TRAILERS

We have access to millions of trailers online. See how the pros put one together. Decide what you enjoy seeing, and then try to do what they are doing. Remember, your film is unique—the trailer should reflect that.

One Thrilling Minute

The trailer has to sell the film, so filmmakers put a lot of time and effort into the making of each one.

66 As an editor who cuts trailers, I can't be concerned with whether the film is great or awful; my job is to create a trailer that shows the potential audience that if they miss this, they'll be missing out on something really special. The thing you cannot do is lie. You don't want to pretend the film is one thing when it is another. 99

—Maureen Nolan
EDITOR, VISUAL EFFECTS SPECIALIST

Finding Your Audience

Hmm, wouldn't it be cool if millions of people saw your film? If you have a good film, social media can help you find a larger audience than you may have ever imagined. You just need to use the internet like a pro.

SOCIAL NETWORKS—THEY CAN BE GOOD FOR BUSINESS

The online universe can be a friendly environment where loads of people get exposed to your film. You send your film to all your friends. If they like it, they send it to their friends. And so on and so on. In fact, you might want to think about setting up a dedicated channel or a website.

[THE NAME OF YOUR FILM].COM— CREATING YOUR FILM'S WEBSITE

If you create a website, that's a great place for people to see your film. Or you may want to post only your trailer. It's up to you. A website is somewhere to show your best work, and it's an efficient way to inform people about you and your film. If the site looks good, people will be interested in who you are and what you are doing.

WHAT'S PUBLICITY? WHAT'S EGO?

You do want to get your name out there, but you don't want to come across like you're full of yourself. Making any film is an accomplishment, and making a really good film is certainly something to be proud of. You want people to know that the film is yours, and that yours is the back they should pat. But humility is always a good thing, and it is something that people are attracted to. So anything you put out on the net? Keep it humble.

YOU ARE NOT ALONE IN THE UNIVERSE

There are other people out there just like you: young, smart, passionate, creative. These people are making films, and they want to see what you're doing, too. They may even want to get together to talk shop. So watch everything you can of other people's work. Let people know when you like what you see. Maybe start up a little conversation with them. You never know what good things can come out of these relationships. Maybe you can help someone with his or her film, or maybe you can even work together on a new film.

IT'S ALL ABOUT RELATIONSHIPS

You want to honor your audience by creating the best work you possibly can. And you want to honor other filmmakers by praising them when their work is excellent and giving them helpful feedback no matter the quality of their work. In this way, all your relationships will be positive and constantly growing.

Festivals

Let's face it: no one becomes rich making short films. Sure, they are a blast to make, but they are also an enormous amount of hard work. So what's the payoff?

Festivals are one of the biggest payoffs. I've been to a few with various films, and they have all been fun. I've had the chance to see a lot of films and meet a lot of filmmakers.

Donna O'Brien-Sokic worked for Disney for many years in marketing and publicity. She now teaches at Humber College in Toronto, Canada. Many of her students have their productions screened at festivals. Here, Donna shares her five steps to getting selected at film festivals.

1 Acquire all your stills during the production of your film and select that one image that best exemplifies the mood and tone. Be consistent in the marketing of your short film by using this image on your poster, postcards, and DVD cover.

2 Identify the marketable elements of your film. These are specific details that make your film unique; they will help you determine exactly what your festival and marketing strategy should be. Marketable elements include star actors, genre, themes, targeted demographic groups, special effects, locations, etc.

3 Use the marketable elements to identify festivals for which your film is suitable. Use Withoutabox (a website that helps independent filmmakers apply to festivals around the world) and search by categories, including genre, theme, student, region, and length. You can also upload your marketing materials to Withoutabox for a festival to access if it chooses your film.

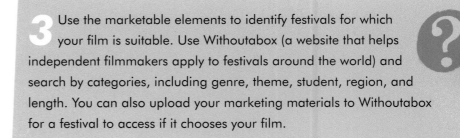

4 Ask yourself if your film has what it takes to get selected at local, national, or international festivals. Be honest with yourself! Make a list of all the festivals for which your film will qualify and note how much it would cost to enter them. Create a marketing budget (don't forget about courier/priority post fees!). Refine your strategy to fit your budget. More and more festivals are now accepting submissions via the video-sharing website Vimeo. This is an extremely cost-effective way to submit your work, and it saves you the costs of DVDs, cases, and postage fees!

5 Don't forget to offer each festival programmer something exclusive about your film. This could be a world premiere, a North American premiere, or a national or local premiere. You could offer exclusive photography from your film—that is, photographs that have never been used before to promote your film. Everyone loves exclusives, and festival programmers are no different!

YOU'RE A STUDENT
—THAT MEANS YOU GET SPECIAL TREATMENT

There are a lot of great festivals for students and a lot that have student competitions. They often don't charge to enter. But remember: it will still cost you some money for materials. Organizers want multiple copies of your film, information about you, posters, one-sheets, and the EPK, so make sure you still have a budget for this.

Your Name in Lights

How can you get your film seen by as many people as possible? An exciting place to start is by entering a film festival.

66 Going to film festivals is the most amazing experience for a filmmaker. Everyone is interested in your film, you are in the frenzy of a happening film event, and you can say, "My film is in the festival!" **99**

—Eva Ziemsen
DIRECTOR, WRITER
A CONVERSATION WITH LARS VON TRIER

It's about Sharing

Making films is about sharing stories, experiences, and emotions. I'm happy to say that I've shared just about everything I know about film with you. I'm also happy to say that I never stop learning: from the filmmakers I work with, from the films I watch, and especially, from the student filmmakers I teach. I feel very lucky to be in a position to share. I've done a lot in my professional life, and I'm hoping to do more. It is my hope that you will share your films. That would be exciting for you and gratifying for your audiences. It wouldn't surprise me if at some point you share your films with me. And undoubtedly, I shall enjoy them and learn something from them. What a joy that will be!

ROLL THE CREDITS!

There are two kinds of people: those who watch film credits (usually filmmakers) and those who don't. There is a lot of information in the credits, including a list of everyone who has worked on the film in any and every capacity.

CAMERA DEPARTMENT
The Eyes behind the Lenses

This department is not only about cameras; it also involves lighting. Many people don't realize how crucial lighting is and how much time and energy it takes. Every image, every frame on the screen must be lit. A scene without specific lighting looks lifeless. The actors don't look very good and neither does anything else. But with proper lighting, the set and the scene come alive. No movies are filmed without lighting. It's that important!

Director of Photography (the DP)

Every department has a head (or boss) and the director of photography is in charge of the fine art of lighting everything that goes in front of the camera as well as the camera work itself.

Gaffer

Whereas the DP decides how the lighting should look, the gaffer actually maneuvers the lights physically. Whenever people are dealing with lights, there is a lot of electricity, so this crew attends to those issues.

Camera Operator

The DP knows where the camera is going, but it is the camera operator who actually does the framing and maneuvers the camera movements in every shot. Framing and composition are also responsibilities of the operator.

First Assistant Camera/Focus Puller

Complicated cameras demand more than one person to ensure a perfect picture. One element that must always be totally accurate is the focus. That's where the 1st AC/focus puller comes in.

Second Assistant Camera

For feature films, there is always a lot of footage shot, so someone needs to keep track of every frame. That is the job of the 2nd AC: writing "camera reports."

Key Grip, Dolly Grip, Grip

Grips work closely with the camera department. The more complicated the shot (say if a dolly or crane is involved) the more help the grips provide. They also work with the gaffer setting up the camera.

> 66 As a cinematographer, my role is to create the look and the feel of the film. However, my passion and love for the project can encourage every crew member. Together we create wonderful moments on film. I never underestimate the power of a cinematographer to influence the energy on set. 99
>
> —Justin Lovell
> **CINEMATOGRAPHER,** *BEN'S RHAPSODY*

ART DEPARTMENT
Make a Scene

There is nothing that you see in a film that happens by chance. Every location has been carefully chosen for how it will eventually look on screen. The same can be said for how a room is decorated, what clothes a character wears, every actor's hairstyle, and much more. This is all the work of the art department. How something looks translates into emotion, which is what films are all about. That's why the art department is so important.

Production Designer/Art Director

This is the person who is ultimately responsible for the look of everything that goes in front of the camera. So if a room, or a spaceship, or a street in the 17th century needs to be designed, that is their responsibility.

Set Decorator

If you see a bedroom on screen, or a kitchen, or a restaurant, the set decorator has made the decision about each piece of furniture and each fork on the table.

Prop Master

Anything that a character holds is called a prop (short for property). The prop master finds, buys, or builds every prop used in a film.

Costume Designer

Actors aren't told to simply bring their own clothes to set. Everything they wear is designed specifically for them and must be in keeping with the role the actor is playing.

Makeup Artist

Actors often work fourteen hours a day under blistering lights. Yet they always look the same in each shot in each scene. How do they manage this? Well, it is the job of the makeup artist to keep them looking consistent from morning until night.

Hair Stylist

Every hairstyle must be appropriate for the character. Even when a character's hair is a mess, it has to be exactly the same mess from shot to shot. That's the job of the stylist.

Special Effects

People are sometimes surprised that special effects are part of the art department. However, special effects are designed for how they will look on screen so they are a natural fit for the art department.

Graphic Designer

Like every other element in a film, the graphics (such as the font of the credits) need to be designed to serve the story. They need to look good and contribute to the film.

Construction Crew

Construction in film is crucial. All the sets have to match what the filmmaker has in mind. And sometimes, when a room is built, each wall must be removable so that the camera can film in every direction.

> 66 On every film, someone decides the look of the environment. If you have the villain sitting in a pink office with a white shag rug, someone has the wrong location or it is a comedy. This work is the most fun for me—designing the sets and locations that give visual references in support of the characters and the story. 99
>
> —Barbara Dunphy
> **PRODUCTION DESIGNER,** *THE MAN WITHOUT A FACE*

PRODUCTION DEPARTMENT
They Keep the Production Running...Smoothly

Even small films are actually very complicated. Locations need to be secured. Equipment must be brought to locations. Cast and crew have to know what is happening when. Every element of the process needs to be clearly planned and tightly coordinated. This is done with really great communication and, as they say in the business, "paperwork." Efficiency is crucial and movie managers are great models of efficiency.

Producer
Although the director actually creates the images, the producer is responsible for the entire project. It's a big job: from securing the script and hiring the director to making sure the film comes in on budget, this person must know about every facet of filmmaking.

Production Manager
Aside from a lot of work on budgeting, the production manager's job is to get anything that needs to be used in filming to the location when it needs to be there.

Location Manager

Every place a film is shot is called a location. It is the location manager's job to find great locations that look good on camera and are accessible to a crew.

First Assistant Director

The assistant director runs the set so the director can focus on the key creative decisions. Basically, the assistant director must solve problem after problem.

Second Assistant Director

On large films, a second assistant director is sometimes necessary, especially if there are a lot of extras in a scene.

Script Supervisor/Continuity

Have you ever seen a film where in one shot a character has a glass in her right hand and in the next shot it is in her left? That's a continuity error, and it's distracting, right? The script supervisor tries to ensure that never happens.

Production Coordinator

Getting people to set when they are supposed to be there can be a major job. The production coordinator organizes everything from limousines to airline tickets.

Production Accountant

Every dollar in a production is important. The finances need to be closely monitored. That is what the production accountant does.

Swing Crew Chief

Moving a crew that could number up to a hundred people, along with all the vehicles and equipment, is like moving a small army. Overseeing this complicated exercise is the task of the swing crew chief.

Drivers

Maneuvering eighteen-wheelers that carry equipment worth millions through narrow city streets can be complicated. Well-trained, safe drivers are a part of every big film shoot.

Publicist

Sometimes you'll hear that there's a "buzz" around a film. This is a good thing, and it's up to the publicist to create that buzz.

Stills Photographer

Images from the film are extremely important for marketing. Every film needs a stills photographer on set to take great images.

> "When people think of successful films, they don't usually think, "Ah, great paperwork!" Nevertheless, great communication between people, whether it is verbal, digital, or written, is a crucial component of every successful film."
>
> —Donna O'Brien-Sokic
> **PRODUCER**

SOUND DEPARTMENT
Heard Any Good Movies Lately?

Well before the cameras roll, filmmakers are making decisions about sound: how to record the sound, what qualities the sound should have, and how the sound will be integrated with the picture. Sound is a major component of the film experience. From the tonal qualities of the dialogue to the music used in the soundtrack, a lot of thought and energy is put into it.

Sound Designer

With the film's director, the sound designer makes a lot of decisions about sound long before the shooting begins. These decisions affect how sound is integrated into the story.

Production Sound Mixer

This is the person who ensures that everything—from the dialogue to the background sounds—is being recorded at the proper levels.

Boom Operator

The best way to record dialogue is still with a microphone at the end of a long pole (a boom mic). The person who physically moves that pole around is the boom operator.

Don't Forget…

In the past few pages, I've listed many core positions on a film crew. But there are many more that are less heralded. We won't list them all but here are a couple of people that are key to a film's success and who are sometimes overlooked.

Composer

The composer creates all the original music for the entire film. Often the composer begins this work after first reading the script and does not finish until the end of postproduction.

Catering

Every day, from morning to night, the craft services people feed the cast and crew. What could be more important? There is nothing like great food on a set to keep everyone happy and productive despite the long hours.

> 66 While there are almost endless opportunities to fix, enhance, and create the visual elements of a film during the postproduction process, there is still no postproduction substitute for clean dialogue that has been well recorded during the initial production. This can save a lot of time and money in postproduction. 99
>
> —Eric Cator
>
> **SOUND RECORDIST, EDITOR,** *KEN DANBY: THE ARTIST'S LIFE*

POSTPRODUCTION DEPARTMENT
Wrap It Up!

At the end of a shoot, a lot of people can finally relax. However, that is the time when an entirely new crew is beginning its many months of work. And, of course, what they do is as important as the filming itself. The postproduction crew must now take the footage and actually create a film. Although there is a lot of technology involved in postproduction, this is an extremely creative time in the making of any film.

Postproduction Supervisor

This is the person who oversees the smooth operation of all the post processes; from booking the facilities and actors when necessary to coordinating the various departments as needed.

Picture Editor

This is the person who works with the director on all editorial decisions and color correction, which means subtly altering the color in many scenes.

Assistant Picture Editor (APE)

This person has the huge job of logging and capturing all the filmed footage. As well, the APE synchronizes the sound recordings to video as needed and maintains a backup system.

Dialogue Editor

This sound editor assembles the finished dialogue tracks and prepares the Automated Dialogue Replacement (ADR) script while working with the ADR recording department.

Visual Effects Coordinator

Visual Effects (VFX) is often a major component of a film. The coordinator works with the director on effects design and, with the VFX crew, executes the effects and the titles.

Supervising Sound Editor

Sound is a huge department in postproduction. This is the person who oversees the smooth operation of all facets of the post sound department.

Music Editor

This sound editor is specifically involved in editing the music to the picture. The rhythm of the music must be in synch with the rhythm of the edits.

Sound Effects Editor

This person plans and executes the sound effects in conjunction with the Foley department.

Foley Editor

The Foley department plans and records the sound effects for on-screen actions when the location recording is not usable.

ADR Editor

Working with the dialogue editor, the ADR editor plans the recording session and works with the actors on getting great performances on lines that must be recorded in postproduction.

Mixer

This person needs to have very sensitive ears. The mixer mixes all the elements of the final soundtrack. This is a very delicate and time-consuming job.

> 66 Once the film has been shot, postproduction takes over, reefing the visuals and sounds captured on set, and adding new elements to sweeten the deal. The postproduction team may be spread out across the city, or even across the country, and a top-notch postproduction coordinator makes all the difference in the world. 99
>
> —Steve Sauve
> **SOUND EDITOR**

Quick Search

A SPECIAL FILM INDEX FOR YOU TO USE

Acknowledgments: To my fellow filmmakers who helped me with this book: Eva Ziemsen, Devon Burns, Mark Achtenberg, Katrina Saville, Eric Cator, David Cadiz, Ashley Bowes, Larry Cohen, Mazi Khalighi, Michelle Latimer, Maureen Nolan, Donna O'Brien-Sokic, Katie Halliday, Steve Sauve, and Bob Richardson. A major thank you to Jessica Burgess, John Crossingham, and the people at Owlkids Books. Another major thank you to Jeff Kulak. And an additional thank you to all the students I have taught over the years: you have helped me to learn.